Masters of
VICTORIAN
PHOTOGRAPHY

Masters of VICTORIAN PHOTOGRAPHY

John Hannavy

David & Charles
Newton Abbot · London · Vancouver

ISBN 0 7153 7032 4

Set in 10 on 12 Goudy
and printed in Great Britain
by The Alden Press, Oxford
for David & Charles (Publishers) Limited
Brunel House Newton Abbot Devon

Published in Canada
by Douglas David & Charles Limited
1875 Welch Street North Vancouver BC

First published in Australia 1976
by Ure, Smith, Sydney
a division of Books for Pleasure Pty Ltd
176 South Creek Road, Dee Why West, Australia 2099

National Library of Australia Card Number and
ISBN 0 7254 0315 2

Contents

Preface

The aim of this volume is to present a sketchbook, or scrapbook, of Victorian photography through which an outline of the scientific, commercial and artistic advances being made at the time can be obtained. By virtue of its size, the book deals only with the work of a few of the most important early British photographers. Their work is discussed in relation to either commercial or aesthetic trends and, in Part Two of the book, short biographical accounts of the photographers are provided.

No book on the history of photography is possible without the help and co-operation of a great many people, to all of whom I am grateful. In particular my thanks are due to John Ward of the Science Museum, London, Philip Hepworth (Norwich Divisional Librarian, Norfolk County Library), the staffs at Aberdeen and Edinburgh City Libraries, and to my wife, Eileen whose assistance has, as usual, been invaluable.

John Hannavy

Part One: The Photograph
The Origins of Photography

The camera obscura had been a useful tool of the artist long before the advent of photography. This simple piece of equipment enabled the artist to trace an image from nature and use it as the basis of a painting. For many decades before the first successful experiments, inventors had toyed with the idea of 'fixing' the camera obscura image and doing away with the laborious job of tracing it. The camera obscura, historically, was any system of projecting an image from nature on to a wall, a board or a translucent screen. In its simplest form it was a darkened room with a small hole in one wall. This acted as a large pinhole camera, projecting the image of the countryside outside on to the opposite wall of the room. This capability of light had been known to scientists and artists for centuries.

In Britain the first potentially successful experiments had been carried out by Thomas Wedgwood, of the pottery family. His interest in preserving the image from the camera obscura was aimed at simplifying the task of producing a huge dinner service for the Czar of Russia. That service was to be adorned with images of the country houses and castles of England, and the royal customer wished to have a different image on each of several hundred pieces. The task was enormous and it was obvious to Wedgwood that some mechanical method of tracing the camera obscura image would greatly reduce his workload. With Humphrey Davy (of safety-lamp fame) he began a series of experiments in chemistry aimed at doing just that. The blackening of silver nitrate when exposed to light had, like the camera, been known for a long time and this formed the basis of his experiments.

Both Wedgwood and Davy had a sound knowledge of chemistry, a training that is reflected in their earliest experiments. Wedgwood began his work using silver nitrate, known to be light sensitive, coated on to leather. He found leather more suitable than paper as it seemed the silver nitrate was more sensitive on that base. (Although he does not appear to have noted the fact, this was owing to the presence of gallic acid in the leather). Davy confined his work to experiments with silver chloride, also sensitive to light. Their work seems to have been rather limited in its scope and their perseverance rather less than it ought to have been for two highly trained chemists. Their early experiments with the camera obscura failed to produce anything. Had they merely extended their exposure times photography might have been invented in 1802 instead of twenty-five years later. Their work on copying tracings was more successful and here they did manage to produce images. However, as they knew of no method of arresting the blackening effect of light, they concluded that the images must be kept in the dark. That conclusion was arrived at far too easily. With papers already

1 Portrait of Niepce

published telling of the 'fixing' effect of ammonia, not to mention common salt, their researches do not seem to have been too thorough. Many writers point out that if two untrained workers in later years, Talbot and Daguerre, could both come up with the idea of common salt as a means of washing away the unblackened silver nitrate, then two chemists of the standing of Wedgwood and Davy should have found that conclusion well within their powers.

They did note in one of their reports that the images produced in their attempts to copy tracings did not really resemble the originals. The reason,

2　Niepce's first photograph

of course, was that the lights and shades were reversed — they had produced
a photographic negative. The year was 1802 and, despite the pioneering work
of Niepce, it was to be over thirty years before the negative would be introduced into the vocabulary of photography.

Let us now turn our attention to the work of Joseph Nicephore Niepce,
to whom history has given the credit for the invention of photography.

The earliest known photograph produced by Niepce is now world famous
and needs little description. Taken from the attic window of his house at
Chalon-sur-Saone the view of his courtyard was produced with an exposure
in excess of eight hours. Its importance historically as the world's first known
photograph is indisputable. However, like the daguerreotype which followed,
it is, in the context of the development of photography as we know it today,
irrelevant.

Niepce used a pewter plate coated with bitumen of Judea as the basis of his
experiments. The bitumen was slightly sensitive to light and became hardened
by the action of that light. After several hours the plate was removed from
the camera and washed in oil of lavender and white spirit which dissolved
the unhardened coating leaving a direct positive image, in hardened bitumen,
on the plate. The hardened areas being white, and the pewter base dark,
the image was unique and could be duplicated only by copying.

Although Niepce referred to this image as his first successful photograph,
he had achieved some considerable success earlier in copying engravings
(usually by transmitted light through the original). His first 'photograph
from nature' was probably taken in 1826 (although the centenary of its pro-

3   Louis Jacques Mande Daguerre

4 Daguerreotype Camera

duction was celebrated at Chalon in 1972) and it is likely that his first successful heliograph — his name for copies of engravings — was taken as early as
eight years before. Like Wedgwood before him, Niepce's early experiments
had produced a negative image, but he too had abandoned that line of
research in favour of this highly original pewter-based process. Niepce seems
to have tried almost every possible base, including glass, which would later
be found to be the ideal photographic base. That, like paper, had been
considered and rejected before the bitumen picture was successfully produced
in 1826.

Louis Jacques Mandé Daguerre, a flamboyant Frenchman, was the next
on the scene. His training as an artist and a set-designer for the French
theatre had drawn him into the public eye. His Diorama, an ingenious
entertainment involving mirrors, lights and paintings, had made his name
well known in Paris. The Diorama took Paris by storm. Crowds of visitors
came to marvel at the ingenious effects. With huge canvases, painted on both
sides (one side representing a scene by day, and the other by night) and an
ingenious system of shutters providing direct or transmitted light, Daguerre
entertained thousands to views of huge Gothic churches by day and then,
as if by magic, lit by candlelight for Midnight Mass. The shutters would
move into place, the daylight would vanish from the scene and, slowly, the
light transmitted through the translucent canvas would reveal the midnight
scene — the crowds standing where once there had been none, and the bright
areas of candlelight where once there had been gloom.

11

5 'The Chess Players', an early framed Daguerreotype

At the same time as his rise to fame with the Diorama Daguerre was working on the problem of fixing the image from his camera obscura. His process was based on sensitising a silvered and polished copper plate. There is a charming story of how he found the key to his process — it may be fact, or it may be simply a pleasing fable — in any case it is worth retelling.

Before Daguerre, all attempts at producing a photographic image had been based on the blackening effect of light on silver salts, or, in Niepce's case, the hardening effect of light on bitumen of Judea. Daguerre's early work followed the same principles, with no greater success than his predecessors.

However, after yet another unsuccessful series of attempts, Daguerre placed the exposed but still blank plates in a cupboard in his laboratory to be taken out, cleaned and reused at a later date. Great was the inventor's surprise, and no doubt delight, to discover on that later date that the plates showed clear signs of images. What had caused the image to appear where none had been before, and without any apparent action by light? Daguerre rightly concluded that some chemical, present in vapour form in the cupboard, must have been responsible and, by a lengthy process of elimination, isolated mercury vapour as the cause. Thus, by a legendary stroke of pure luck, the idea of 'development' was introduced into photography. Slowly,

12

6   William Henry Fox Talbot

one by one, the constituents of photography were being discovered and assembled.

Daguerre's image was, like that produced by Niepce, a direct positive (although it could be seen as a negative if viewed by light reflected from a light background). The process was first successfully used by Daguerre and Isidore Niepce in 1837 and, by 1839, was in a sufficiently advanced form to be launched on an eager market.

In sharp contrast to Niepce's process, the Daguerreotype produced an image with an extremely fine grain, a high degree of sharpness and image contrast and, most important, with the introduction of the idea of development, an exposure of between five and thirty minutes. For such a giant step to be made all at once was typical of the evolution of photography, which progressed by enormous leaps and bounds during those early years. Thus photography's first commercially viable process was reasonably quick and of a surprisingly high quality.

But however many advantages the daguerreotype may have had, its disadvantages were equally as significant. Foremost among the latter was the unique quality of the image. The only way a duplicate of a daguerreotype could be achieved was either by taking a second original photograph, or by

13

7   Some of Talbot's early cameras

attempting to copy the first. Actually, thanks to a clever piece of advertising, this uniqueness was promoted as an added advantage — supposedly giving the daguerreotype the same standing as a portrait produced by an artist.

In the meantime, on the other side of the Channel, the British were not idle — or at least one Englishman, William Henry Fox Talbot, the squire of Lacock Abbey, wasn't! Fox Talbot had boundless energy, a great talent for innovation and the ability to think about several different things at the same time. He ran his estates and the large family house at Lacock. The village was almost entirely tied to the house, and consequently the squire was the figurehead of the community and Talbot took his responsibilities seriously. He had interests in physics and chemistry, art and archaeology, literature and history, not to mention politics. That latter interest was channelled into a short political career as the Tory MP for the Chippenham constituency in which Lacock village and Abbey were situated.

Between sessions of Parliament Talbot devoted much of his time to the now familiar problem of 'fixing the image in the camera obscura'. Like so many of the inventors he was an artist who rather liked the idea of simplifying the task of drawing from nature.

Talbot's process was announced in 1840, the year after the daguerreotype, but the two processes were quite different. Apart from their mutual dependence on development the light-sensitive properties of silver salts, and the use of salt as a fixer, they had little in common. By the end of 1840 both inventors were equipped with the knowledge that there was a latent image present on the plate after exposure, which could be made visible by chemical development. We have already seen how Daguerre interpreted this knowledge. Talbot, on the other hand, reverted to Wedgwood's original experiments with paper and produced a 'negative' image from which 'positive' prints could be made. Talbot arrived at the idea of development by as lucky an accident as Daguerre — while he too was trying to re-use material which had failed to produce an image. By resensitising it, the image was immediately developed. Thus the beginning of the 'calotype' or 'Talbotype' process was marked by reduced exposure times. His 'Photogenic Drawing' process had required a long exposure to produce a visible image in the camera which required only fixation.

'Latticed Window
(with the Camera Obscura)
August 1835

When first made, the squares
of glass about 200 in number
could be counted, with help
of a lens.

8 An early '*Photogenic Drawing*' of a lattice window at Lacock, August 1835

Talbot's first successful picture was a 'Photogenic Drawing' of the lattice window at Lacock, reproduced on a tiny piece of sensitised paper about the size of a large postage stamp. Talbot noted that when the picture was taken the panes of glass could be counted, so clear was the image. Talbot's process gave a coarser image than its French rival; but with the advantage of being able to produce countless copies from a single negative, the calotype was bound to succeed.

The calotype marks the true beginning of modern photography, and being an astute businessman he had it covered by very explicit patents which he guarded jealously. With manufacturing processes in the hands of the user, Talbot had to go to great lengths in order to ensure a financial return from his investment. Today, with all manufacturing undertaken by the giant photographic companies, patents merely restrain other companies from using patented ideas. In the early days the photographer coated his own papers. Talbot therefore had to control the use of his process by issuing licences to all potential users. That in itself was quite justified, but Talbot took things rather too far by trying to assert his patent control over all photographic processes which involved the production of a negative and a positive. It was to take some time, and involve several legal actions, before the limits of his patent control were clearly defined. His claim to have patented the idea, rather than the process, would never be allowed today. However, in 1841 and 1842 patents were issued without the tight controls of today. Talbot's patent is, however, one of the most important and interesting documents of early photography, and it is reproduced here in a slightly edited form to remove all the legal niceties with which such documents abound.

The first part of my invention is a method of making paper extremely sensitive to the rays of light. For this purpose I select the best writing paper, having a smooth surface and a close and even texture.

First Part of the Preparation of the Paper
I dissolve one hundred grains of crystallised nitrate of silver in six ounces of distilled water. I wash one side of the paper with this solution with a soft camel hair brush, and place a mark upon that side by which

15

9 Calotype negative and positive by Hill and Adamson. The figure on the left of the positive
is John Henning and, on the right, D. O. Hill

to know it again. I dry the paper cautiously at a distant fire, or else I leave it to dry spontaneously in a dark place. Next I dip the paper in a solution of iodide of potassium, containing five hundred grains of that salt dissolved in one pint of water. I leave the paper a minute or two in this solution. I then take it out and dip it in water, I then dry it lightly with blotting paper and finish drying it at a fire; or else I leave it to dry spontaneously; all this process is best done in the evening by candlelight. The paper thus prepared may be called, for the sake of distinction, 'iodized paper'. This iodized paper is scarcely sensitive to light, but nevertheless, it should be kept in a portfolio or some dark place till wanted for use; it does not spoil by keeping any length of time provided it is kept in a portfolio and not exposed to light.

Second Part of the Preparation of the Paper
This second part is best deferred until the paper is wanted for use; when that time is arrived, I take a sheet of the iodized paper, and wash it with a liquid prepared in the following manner: — Dissolve one hundred grains of crystallized nitrate of silver in two ounces of distilled water, to this solution add one sixth of its volume of strong acetic acid; let this mixture be called A. Dissolve crystallized gallic acid in distilled water as much as it will dissolve (which is a very small quantity); let this solution be called B. When you wish to prepare a sheet of paper for use, mix together the liquids A and B in equal volumes. This mixture I shall call by the name of gallo-nitrate of silver. Let no more be mixed than is intended to be used at one time, because the mixture will not keep good for a long period. Then take a sheet of iodized paper and wash it over with this gallo-nitrate of silver with a soft camel hair brush, taking care to wash it on the side which has been previously

16

marked. This operation should be performed by candlelight. Let the paper rest half a minute, and then dip it into water, then dry it lightly with blotting paper and lastly, dry it cautiously at a fire, holding it a considerable distance therefrom. When dry the paper is fit for use but it is advisable to use it within a few hours after its preparation. (Note that if it is used immediately, the last drying may be dispensed with, and the paper may be used moist). (Note 2nd, instead of a solution of gallic acid for the liquid B, the tincture of galls diluted with water may be used but it is not so advisable.)

Use of the Paper: — The paper thus prepared and which I name 'Calotype Paper' is placed in a camera obscura, so as to receive the image formed in the focus of the lens, of course the paper must be screened or defended from the light during the time it is being put in the camera. When the camera is properly pointed at the object, this screen is withdrawn, or a pair of internal folding doors are opened, so as to expose the paper for the reception of the image. If the object is very bright, or the time employed is sufficiently long, a sensible image is perceived upon the paper when it is withdrawn from the camera. But when the time is short, or the objects dim, no image whatever is visible upon the paper, which appears entirely blank. Nevertheless, it is impressed with an invisible image; and I have discovered the means of causing this image to become visible. This is performed as follows: — I take some gallonitrate of silver, prepared in the manner before directed, and with this liquid I wash the paper all over with a soft camel hair brush, I then hold it before a gentle fire, and, in short time (varying from a few seconds to a minute or two), the image begins to appear upon the paper. Those parts of the paper upon which light has acted most strongly become brown or black while those parts on which light had not acted remain white. The image continues to strengthen and grow more and more visible during some time. When it appears strong enough, the operation should be terminated and the picture fixed.

The Fixing Process: — In order to fix the picture thus obtained, I first dip it into water, I then partly dry it with blotting paper, and then wash it with a solution of bromide of potassium, containing one hundred grains of that salt dissolved in eight or ten ounces of water. The picture is then washed with water and then finally dried. Instead of bromide of potassium a strong solution of common salt may be used but it is less advisable. The picture thus obtained will have the lights and shades reversed with respect to the natural objects; videlicet, the lights of the object are represented by shades and vice versa. But it is easy from this picture to obtain another, which shall be conformable to nature; videlicet, in which the lights shall be represented by lights and the shades by shades. It is only necessary for this purpose to take a second sheet of sensitive calotype paper, and place it in close contact with the first, upon which the picture has been formed. A board is put beneath them, and a sheet of glass above, and the whole is pressed into close contact by screws. Being then placed in sunshine, or daylight, for a short time, an image or copy is formed upon the second sheet of paper.

10   Printing a calotype

11 Foden's workshops in Lacock

This image or copy is often invisible at first, but the image may be made to appear in the same way that has been already stated. But I do not recommend that this copy should be taken on calotype paper, on the contrary, I would advise that it should be taken on common photographic paper. This paper is made by washing good writing paper first with a weak solution of common salt, and next with a solution of nitrate of silver, since it is well known, having been communicated freely to the public by myself, in the year One Thousand eight hundred and thirty-nine, and that it forms no part of the present invention, I need not describe it here more particularly; although it takes a much longer time to obtain a copy upon this paper than upon calotype paper, yet the tints of the copy are generally more harmonious and agreeable. On whatever paper the copy is taken, it should be fixed in the way already described. After a calotype picture has furnished a good many copies, it sometimes grows faint, and the subsequent copies inferior. This may be prevented by means of a process which revives the strength of the calotype pictures. In order to do this, it is only necessary to wash them by candlelight with gallo-nitrate of silver and then warm them. This causes all the shades of the picture to darken considerably, while the white parts are unaffected. After this the picture is, of course, to be fixed a second time. The picture will then yield a second series of copies, and a great number of them may frequently be made.

Thus Talbot provides us with a very full report of his researches and his process. Some of the cameras used for these early experiments were made for him by the village carpenter in Lacock, Joseph Foden, who was frequently called upon by the squire to manufacture odd items of equipment in connection with Talbot's many experiments and interests, both inside and outside photography.

19

12　Joseph Foden

Despite the obvious restrictions placed by Talbot on the use of his process, it did achieve wide success. The Calotype Club, formed in 1847 by a group of photographers licensed by Talbot, did much to promote the advance of the 'black art'. In Scotland, where Talbot's patents held no sway, the calotype, surprisingly, found few devotees. David Octavius Hill and Robert Adamson were the obvious Scottish masters of the process, but photography generally did not catch on until the arrival of the waxed paper process invented by yet another Frenchman, Gustave le Gray.

Before le Gray's arrival on the scene the daguerreotype had reigned supreme in France and, despite the obvious advantages of Talbot's process, the little silvered plate had made considerable inroads into the English market. Through its English patent holder, Richard Beard, licences had been issued to a number of portrait photographers, and Beard himself had opened a highly successful daguerreotype studio at the Royal Polytechnic Institution in London as early as 1841. He soon had several other studios in London, in Parliament Street, and at Nos 31 and 85 King William Street in the City.

A certain rivalry had existed between the two processes ever since their announcement. The uniqueness and fine image quality of the French system opposed the coarser image but easily repeatable 'copy' available from the English invention. Talbot's process had one major disadvantage — the paper texture of the negative was always printed through on to the positive. Daguerre's process had the problem of being unrepeatable, although its clear sharp image was obviously more desirable than the calotype. The search

13   Talbot's glasshouse at Reading

14   Talbot's printing establishment at Reading

15   Barque *Ellen Simpson*, a calotype by Fox Talbot

was now on for a compromise between the two, and the first solution was that put forward by le Gray. He suggested the simple expedient of greasing or waxing the paper before it was sensitised to render it transparent and thus lessen the offending texture. In that form the process attracted many more users, especially as there was a general feeling that the le Gray variant would not be covered by Talbot's patent. Talbot had other ideas, however, and waxed paper users soon found themselves requiring Talbot licences.

There is no doubt that Gustave le Gray based his process on Talbot's, and no doubt either that by doing so he extended the lists of photographers using the process, as well as the life of the process itself, by several years. To the lists of calotype photographers such as Hill, Adamson, Roger Fenton, Talbot himself, and others many new names could now be added, among them were Thomas Keith of Edinburgh, and his brother-in-law John Forbes White.

It was in Frederick Scott Archer's hands that the real future of photography lay. Disappointed by the calotype process taught to him by Dr Hugh Diamond, one of the founder members of the Calotype Club, Archer decided to improve the process himself. Even with the waxed paper version the paper texture was still a problem, and it was that feature of the system which Archer sought to replace. His first ideas revolved around finding a replacement base for the calotype emulsion, and after several experiments he started working with what was then a recent discovery — collodion — a sticky substance formed by dissolving gun-cotton in ether and used at the time for dressing wounds. The collodion dried to form a clear film which Archer thought might serve instead of the paper. His experiments were rather unspectacular until he first tried coating the emulsion, suspended in

22

16 Frederick Scott Archer

23

OBSERVATORY, Cranford, Middlesex.

NORTH LATITUDE........ 51° 28′ 57.8″
Min. Sec.
WEST LONGITUDE......... 1 37.5

ENLARGED PHOTOGRAPHIC COPY

OF A PHOTOGRAPH OF

THE MOON

HOUR
SEPTEMBER 7, 1857, 14—15

The Original Collodion Positive was obtained in five seconds,
by means of a Newtonian Equatoreal of thirteen inches
aperture and ten feet focal length.

Sir John W. Herschel Bart.
with Warren De la Rue's
Compliments

Sept 22/57

17 'The Moon', a wet collodion picture by Warren de la Rue

collodion, on to that clearest of all supports, glass. Here was the ultimate in texture-free bases. Initial experiments with a dry plate coated with the collodion and silver salts showed little sensitivity but, if the plate was exposed wet, the sensitivity was high and the quality quite good. (Archer's first successes with the collodion process involved using the glass merely as a support for coating and producing a light-sensitive collodion film. When dry the film was peeled off the glass support and exposed in the camera. The thickness of the collodion needed, and the resultant opacity, led him to start out on the successful series of tests which led to the glass becoming an integral part of the negative material.)

Archer sought no financial reward from his process and offered it free and without condition to anyone who wished to use it. He took out no patents and, apart from publishing a number of papers, he did little to associate his own name with the process. He did comment to a friend, a few years after his original announcement, that he wished he had called the process the archertype. That wish was probably prompted by his disgust at the claims and counterclaims which were made by other would-be inventors, each wishing to claim the wet-plate process as his own. Even Fox Talbot, still working under a gross misconception of what his patent rights were, tried to suppress the free use of the collodion plate, claiming it was subject to his control. Several photographers bowed to Talbot's might before one, Silvester Laroche, took the case to court in 1854, three years after Archer's original description of the process.

With Talbot's rights clearly defined for the first time as a result of the Talbot v Laroche legal battle, the patents on both the daguerreotype and the calotype were allowed to lapse. As the wet-plate process gave better quality than the calotype and coupled the high quality of the daguerreotype with the facility for multiple 'copying' or printing, the early processes were destined to fade out within as few years, at least in Britain. In America the life of the daguerreotype seems to have been a little longer.

The free availability of a fairly sophisticated photographic process was the signal for a tremendous growth in the use of the medium. By 1853 a Photographic Society had been formed by several of the original members of the Calotype Club, and the infant society was attracting a large and cosmopolitan membership. That society went from strength to strength until it grew into the Royal Photographic Society of today.

The three early processes continued to be used alongside the new wet-plate process for a few years, but after about 1855 or 1856 Archer's process seems to have reigned supreme. For a time at least it relied on Talbot's original salted printing paper, described in his early patents, for the production of prints, although the albumen printing paper process had been introduced in 1850/1. Just as the wet plate took a few years to establish itself and oust its rivals, so it was with Blanquart–Evrard's printing paper.

Albumen paper, as its name might suggest, used the whites of eggs to bind the light sensitive silver halides to the paper. The process is interesting both for the advance in print quality which it brought to photographers and because, for the first time, at least part of the production of a photographic material was taken out of the photographer's hands. The old salted paper as detailed by Talbot had to be prepared entirely by the photographer. With the albumen process, however, several brands of paper, already coated with the egg white, soon appeared on the market. The photographer had then to soak the paper in a solution of common salt and sensitise it with silver nitrate before drying it in the dark and using it. The paper was a 'printing-out-paper' — that is, the photographer waited until prolonged exposure to light caused a contact print to appear without development.

Shortly after the introduction of the wet plate several brands of prepared collodion also appeared on the market but, as the plates had to be exposed while the emulsion was still damp, their manufacture was always the task of the photographer.

This tended to make the lot of the wet-plate photographer rather a difficult one. He not only had to carry his often large camera around with him — but also a portable darkroom or dark tent. He would pose his picture, retire into his tent to coat his plate and hope that his subjects did not move. The sequence of events in the manufacture of a collodion plate was fairly time-consuming. First the photographer cleaned his glass, then coated it with a solution of collodion in which an amount of potassium iodide has been dissolved. This thick gluey substance was poured on to the centre of the glass plate which was then tilted in every direction to ensure an even coating. Uneven collodion, or too thick a layer of the material, was the cause of many a spoiled picture. The coated plate was then sensitised in a bath of silver nitrate — the nitrate bath about which so much was written, and so many photographers complained, during the wet-plate era. The plate was then placed in a dark slide, carried to the camera, exposed and then, back in the tent, developed, all before the emulsion had a chance to dry. If it did dry then the collodion would, at worst, crack and, at best, become too insensitive to produce the image in a sufficiently short exposure time. The eight hours of Niepce's exposure for that original pewter plate had been reduced to between two and twenty seconds by the wet-plate era. Two seconds, however, as many photographers found to their cost, is long enough for people to move a considerable distance. In portraiture, head clamps were used to aid the sitters in remaining quite still, and photographers in the field developed unique skills of posing, using every possible position in which the human body could be kept still without strain, while retaining a casual 'un-posed' appearance.

With the wet plate firmly established, the scene was now set for the emergence of some of the finest photographers Britain has ever produced.

The wet-plate survived until the 1880s when a dry version of the gelatine system replaced it. The dry plate, with its short exposure time and the facility for preparing the plate long before it was needed, freed the photographer from many of the restrictions of the earlier days. He no longer needed his dark tent, and therefore no longer required his subjects to sit still while he made his plates. Pictures could now reflect a much more natural approach. The dry plate also heralded the beginnings of the mass production of photographic materials.

In 1888 the advent of the roll film camera started the modern revolution in photography towards the sophisticated processes we enjoy today.

Commercial Trends

From its earliest moments the commercial potential of photography had been in the forefront of the minds of its inventors and users. Daguerre and Talbot, responsible for the first two viable systems, were both acutely aware of the capital which could be made out of their inventions. As has been seen, both sought patents protecting their rights and giving them the authority to licence all users. The two processes were obvious successes in portraiture and it was from these early uses that both men gained the first returns on their labours.

In France the daguerreotype studios began to spring up all over the fashionable districts of Paris, while in Britain daguerreotype studios had to compete for sites and custom with the calotype establishments licensed by Talbot or his agents.

It is not clear if Daguerre himself became involved in the commercial practice of photography, but, judging by the photographs which still exist of his printing establishment at Reading, Fox Talbot certainly did.

Talbot himself pioneered many of the uses of photography, portraiture and architecture were but two of his fields, and he realised early on the appeal of illustrated books. In 1844 he published *The Pencil of Nature* and followed this the next year with *Sun Pictures in Scotland*. They were both instantly successful.

One of the first commercial uses of the new medium was the epic task, undertaken by David Octavius Hill and Robert Adamson, producing the mammoth painting of the First General Assembly of the Free Church of Scotland. To assist in the task of painting the faces of the many clergy in the picture, Hill and Adamson first photographed the ministers, either singly or in groups, and, working from the calotype prints, later copied them on to the canvas. The exactness of the copies is uncanny. Hill incorporated himself in the painting and is seen on the right of the picture with a simple calotype camera. The Signing of the Act of Separation and Deed of Demission at Tanfield in Edinburgh was carried out in May 1843, but it took Hill and Adamson several months to complete the photography, and it was to be several years before the painting was completed.

At that time Hill was still working as an artist and this work is perhaps the first instance of the use of photography as something besides an end in in itself. It is interesting to note that this early commercial application of the process brought no financial return for the inventor whose patents, as already mentioned, did not extend to Scotland.

By the late 1840s there were numerous professional photographic establishments in the major cities. Portrait photography was by far the most

18   Princes Street, Edinburgh, an instantaneous picture by George Washington Wilson

common application and prices were high. The time-consuming task of
making the calotype or daguerreotype materials, long exposures and the
need for almost immediate processing limited the photographer's possible
daily output and pushed prices up.

With the advent of the wet plate, which allowed photographers a little
more scope by giving them the means of producing finer quality images and
the facility for producing numerous prints, the uses of photography spread
quickly. The wet-plate photographer was still hindered, however, by the
length of time needed to take and process a single picture. In an average day
a photographer might take no more than four or five pictures.

The wet-plate process did allow him to make a greater return on his work.

28

19 Head of Roman Boy, British Museum, an early commercial photograph taken for the Museum Trustees by Roger Fenton

29

By producing a long run of prints and marketing them through one of a number of publishing houses, which sprang up almost overnight, he could reach a larger public and reduce the cost per print. We are lucky to have a number of invoices from the 1850s which reveal the high cost of photography. Ignoring inflation, the current reduced value of the pound and all the other variables, the cost of a photograph in 1858 was greater than it is today.

Several of the publishing houses became very well known — Williams & Co of New York, Moulin of Paris, Colnaghi of London, and Thomas Agnew of Manchester being four of the most enterprising. To that list could be added the De la Rue company, the Francis Frith print publishing concern in Reigate and George Washington Wilson's factories in Aberdeen which, although later on the scene, went on to become the largest photographic publishing concern in Europe, and perhaps even in the world.

By the time of the outbreak of the Crimean War in 1854 at least the first four of these companies were in operation, for they undertook the marketing of Roger Fenton's series of pictures of the war. It should be added, though, that all four were originally formed as print and engraving publishers and later became involved with photography. Prices for Fenton's Crimean studies ranged from half a guinea to a guinea each and the price for the 'complete work' of 160 pictures was 60 guineas.

From Fenton and his rival Francis Bedford we have examples of the pricing of photography in those early days. Bedford supplied an invoice to the Privy Purse for eleven prints (contacts) from existing negatives at 3s each in 1863. Fenton's invoice to the Privy Purse as early as 1854 showed that his prints cost 1s 6d each and 2s for a slightly larger size. His negatives cost 1 guinea each. For some reason, in that invoice, Fenton prices prints of 'The Fleet at Anchor' at 7s 6d each.

By May of the same year, in his dealings with the British Museum, Fenton offered five negative sizes priced at 10s, 11s, 12s 6d and 15s each, with the largest size priced at 1 guinea. Prints from these cost 1s, 1s 3d, 1s 6d and 2s 6d, with the two smallest sizes costing the same. By the time he wrote a letter to the Museum trustees on 24 October 1857, he was charging 2 guineas if the picture was taken in sunlight outside, and a phenomenal 4 guineas if the picture had to be taken indoors. The prints from the 15in square plates were to cost 2s each and had to be bought by the hundred, at £10.

These prices were only possible because there were relatively few photographers and their daily output had to be small. If photography was to become cheap some public involvement with the medium had to be generated, increasing the demand for photography and thereby, hopefully, reducing prices. That public involvement came with photography's first 'craze' in the 1850s when the stereoscope was launched on to the market. Stereoscopic photography was a relatively early arrival on to the photographic scene, and, with the development of small cameras, easily portable and quick to use, the production of stereo view-cards became part of almost every professional photographer's life.

Stereoscopic vision, upon which three-dimensional photography is based, had been known to man long before photography became a reality. The first recorded observations that our two eyes each see a different image is attributed

20 Hurst Green, also by Fenton, is typical of the type of print which was bought by the
Victorians for framing and hanging on the drawing room wall

21 HMS *Cambridge* in the Hamoaze; great gun practice. An instantaneous picture by
George Washington Wilson. The smoke surprised the print-buying public who had
never seen action 'frozen' by the camera before

22   Advertisement for a hand stereo viewer

to Euclid in 300 BC, and the same observation was made in the first century AD by Ptolemy. One of the most detailed investigations into the phenomena was made in the sixteenth century by Leonardo de Vinci who noticed that, because of the different relative positions of the eyes in respect to the subject, their views of it would be different.

In the nineteenth century, working on these early observations, Charles Wheatstone carefully drew images of a subject viewed first by the left eye and then by the right. With an ingenious construction of mirrors he viewed the left-hand drawing with the left eye and, simultaneously, the other drawing with his right eye. His work was rewarded when he realised that he was viewing a three dimensional representation of the subject. His stereoscopic viewer was later used for viewing pairs of photographic images taken to simulate the views obtained by the two eyes. This was achieved by setting up the camera, taking one picture, moving the camera laterally by the distance between the centres of the human eyes — about $2\frac{1}{2}$in — and then taking the second. The two pictures could then be 'united' in the Wheatstone stereoscope to produce a three-dimensional image.

However, the pictures required for the Wheatstone apparatus were large, and it was not until the introduction of a small format and a miniature camera and viewer that the idea really caught on. The small stereo camera and the viewer to take the resultant pictures were the work of Sir David Brewster and J. B. Dancer, whose pioneering work in the field of stereo equipment set the pattern for generations to come. The size which became standard was about $2\frac{1}{2}$in square with a similar distance between the centres of the pictures.

Although the stereo format had been tried with the daguerreotype, the

23 'Fruit Flowers and Parian Vase' — a stereo pair by Fenton

24 In this stereo pair, the two figures only appear in the right frame. Stereo pictures were originally taken in sequence rather than together. The camera was designed to allow the plate to be moved between exposures

calotype and the waxed paper process, it was not until the advent of the simple duplication combination of collodion plate and albumen paper, that the commercial exploitation of the idea was really possible.

Almost overnight the stereo craze arrived. In 1858 the *Stereoscopic Magazine*, published by Lovell Reeve, first appeared on the scene. At 2s 6d per issue, containing three pairs of stereo pictures, it was expensive, but its survival for almost five years is proof of its success. It was followed by the *Stereoscopic Cabinet* at the same price containing three stereo cards in a presentation wallet. Books illustrated with stereo pictures soon followed, *The Conway in the Stereoscope*, written by J. B. Davidson and illustrated by Fenton (who was one of the first to jump on the stereoscopic bandwagon) was one of the most successful.

Many new companies appeared on the scene to cash in on the new craze. Many of them did not last for long but the best, among them the London Stereoscopic and Photographic Company, went from strength to strength and adapted their output to suit the varying tastes of the Victorian public. Most of the already established photographers found that they had to adapt

25   A Victorian *carte-de-visite*

in order to survive and began producing stereo cards, often for publication by Lovell Reeve, but also for publication through the already established print publishers, and a number of new arrivals on the scene.

It was the demand for stereoscopic viewcards which established George Washington Wilson of Aberdeen. He was one of the masters of the small format and his pictures were always well reviewed by the photographic press. Francis Bedford and Roger Fenton, who have already figured in this story, also became prolific producers of stereoscopic views. Bedford worked along the well-trodden photographic routes of North Wales — as did so many

26   A family group photographed by J. Rae of Dumfries

others that their tripod holes must have been permanently visible in the soil! Much of Fenton's material was marketed through Reeve who, in addition to the magazine and the *Cabinet*, had published the Davidson book. He also marketed a series of sets of view cards at a guinea for fifteen views.

Prices had dropped considerably and the small stereo cards now cost less than 2s each. The professionally produced portrait, however, was still expensive and, therefore, still a luxury only available to the middle and upper classes.

Photography for the masses was the next target for those who directed the fortunes of the 'black art'. The nineteenth century was a century of formality, of introductions before one person could speak to another, and of visiting cards to be presented to the butler or maid when calling upon a friend. Disderi of Paris, in 1859, popularised the idea of the small portrait, no bigger than a visiting card. The *carte-de-visite* photograph was born. The format was small and the cost could be as low as a few pennies.

It is probable that Disderi envisaged the use of the little picture merely as an inexpensive portrait and visiting card. However, the picture-buying public saw it differently. Within a very short space of time people began exchanging *cartes* and building up collections of portraits of their friends. To these collections were soon added commercially produced and marketed portraits of celebrities — royalty, politicians and church dignitaries. As demand grew so did competition. Prices fell sharply and the demand for the large format landscape picture or portrait almost died out. Many of the photographers of the period adapted, but many more, whose working criterion was quality and not quantity, found that they could not produce work of a sufficiently high quality within the expected price range. Fenton left photography, Bedford continued to produce illustrations for books and

27 The family album, containing both *cartes-de-visite* and cabinet prints, was often embellished with hand-printed decoration

Frith devoted his time almost exclusively to publishing. Others like William Lake Price, whose *Manual of Photographic Manipulation* was a standard text of the period, tried to combine the two by producing *cartes-de-visite* at the expected price to provide a living, while at the same time continuing to produce large format material to satisfy their own high standards.

The London Stereoscopic and Photographic Company abandoned all but a fraction of its output of stereo cards and became one of the largest producers of *cartes-de-visite* in the world. Their catalogue included almost every well-known figure in Britain; they also photographed most of Europe's royalty and the President of the United States, Abraham Lincoln.

There was, no doubt, some degree of collaboration between the leading producers in Britain, France and America, as the products of French studios, among them those of the pioneer Disderi, appeared on the British market. In a smaller way George Washington Wilson also made inroads into the *cartes* market.

The market for cheap portraits was satisfied by literally thousands of small local studios equipped with cameras capable of taking several portraits on a single plate. With this simple facility a number of negatives could be processed and printed at one time, leaving the photographer free to spend more time actually taking pictures and therefore earning money. There is no doubt that by the early 1860s the photographic market in Britain had reached saturation point. The demand for the *carte-de-visite* lasted a few years so most were rewarded for their work.

By the later 1860s demand was on the wane and a new format was created to counter dwindling sales — the 'Cabinet' picture. This was about twice the size of the *carte-de-visite* and was produced on the same mass-production basis as its predecessor. However, although it remained in fashion until the

28   *Cartes-de-visite* prints displayed in a folding leather frame

29   As the craze grew, the backs of the mounts became more and more ornate

30   One of the many portraits of Church dignitaries sold as *cartes-de-visite*, was this 1862
portrait of Cardinal Wiseman

31 This cabinet print displays all the photographer's many successes

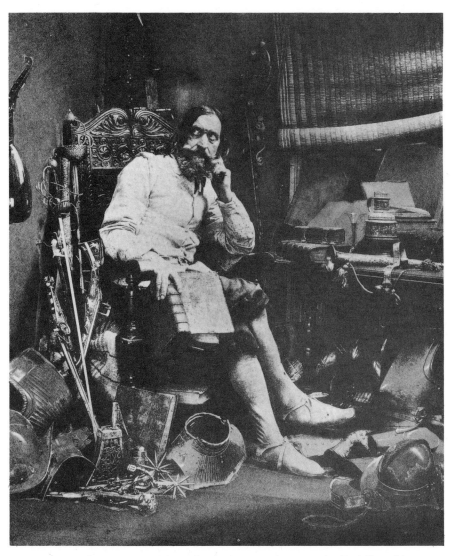

32 'Don Quixote in His Study', a photo-galvanographic print by Paul Pretsch's patent
process, from a photograph by Lake Price

turn of the century, continuing to be produced through the demise of the
wet plate and its replacement by the dry plate and gelatin plate, it never
achieved the universal appeal that was hoped for. However, the precedent
of cheap portraits had been created and sustained for over a quarter of a
century. It lasted until the advent of the roll-film camera, introduced by
Kodak in the late 1880s, marked the beginnings of amateur photography as
we know it today. That innovation — photography for all — while setting
the pattern for photography for a century, was a near-fatal blow for professional portraiture from which it is still recovering.

Other commercial ventures involving photography were conceived
throughout the nineteenth century. Many of them involved systems for the
photo-mechanical reproduction of photographs which would be offered for

33 York Minster from Lendall, a photo-galvanographic print from a picture by Fenton

sale to the public. The first of these was the Photo-Galvanographic process developed by Paul Pretsch in the 1850s. Pretsch evolved a process based on the principles of the collodion system but taken a step further, so that the plate could be reticulated, causing the gelatin to accept water in varying degrees in relation to the image depth. The plate could then be used as a mould for the production of a copper printing plate from which a limited number of prints could be made. The process was launched in 1856 and achieved a limited success. Fenton was the company's chief photographer — that man had a knack of being in the forefront of every new development in photography during his short professional career — and a number of the photographs reproduced by the process were, therefore, his work. However, the work of Lake Price, Cundall and Howlett (two portrait photographers who rose to fame during the Crimean War) and a landscape photographer called Lebbin Colls was also featured. Prints were issued in three qualities, dependent on the state of the plate at the time they were pulled. The plate deteriorated quickly so the first prints — 'Choice Proofs', were the best quality, followed by 'Proofs' and then 'Prints'. Prices varied according to quality and ranged from 10s 6d, through 7s 6d to 5s for 'Prints'.

The short life of the process does not in any way reduce its importance as being the first practical system of photo reproduction. It was on the pioneering work of Fox Talbot's photoglyphy process and Pretsch's system that the subsequent reproduction systems were based. (It should be added here that Talbot's patents for his own process were used by him, often successfully, to suppress the publication of Pretsch's prints, until, in another legal action, Talbot was once more made aware of the limits of his patents!) It was quite some time after Pretsch's company had gone into liquidation before the practice of illustrating books with hand-made photographic prints was replaced by a mechanical system of photo-engraving.

Pretsch's commercial ventures with the process produced the beautiful *Photographic Art Treasures*, a monthly series of prints published in 1856 and intermittently for a couple of years. Other more ambitious projects never seem to have got past the planning stage. Early prints were heavily retouched by hand, but the need for all this afterwork seems to have been eliminated while the Photo-Galvanographic Company was still in its infancy. In later publications, a fourth quality of print was offered — in the 'Print' quality, but coloured, at 7s 6d per print. Neither of the two better qualities was ever offered coloured.

Artistic Trends

In setting out to chronicle the artistic trends in Victorian photography, the writer must find himself with something of a problem. So much of the material already published on the artistic merits of the work of the pioneers is based on the misconception that their criteria for judging artistic, rather than technical, quality were the same as ours. By omission rather than design, writers have credited some of the early photographers with the ability to seek out, rather than merely tolerate, some of the characteristics of the processes at their disposal. That is not to say that all the finest products of the Victorian camera were nothing more than fortuitous accidents. There were many photographers, from the earliest days of the calotype, whose work achieved great artistic heights. These, however, were the exceptions rather than the rule and much of the material produced was not, and still is not, worthy of mention.

Those photographers whose work did achieve any degree of artistic merit were usually those whose pre-photographic background had been in the world of the fine arts. As the subject advanced through the second half of the nineteenth century the number of good picture-makers, who were not merely technically good photographers increased. These were the lucky ones who by virtue of their later arrival on the scene, could learn from and build on the successes of their predecessors.

In the infancy of photography, little more was expected of the process than the production of a recognisable likeness to the view or the person before the camera. With the crude processes and equipment little more was possible. But progress in photography was made at such a phenomenal rate that it was not long before the first true works of art had been produced.

As one process was replaced by another a little more refined, so the craving for better technical quality — finer detail, sharper images — became the accepted attitude of the photographer. Very few photographers exploited the granular image of the calotype or the waxed paper process, which were both succeeded by the clearer collodion plate. Even with collodion, capable of some quite unusual effects on occasions, the photograph was praised only if the recorded image was faithful to the original subject. Unless maximum detail was present the pictures were only given grudging approval by the photographic press and the completely uninspired critics of the *Illustrated London News* and other widely read journals. In the cases where a particular process was used to good creative effect, it was often alongside a more conventional use. Thus David Octavius Hill, while producing his excellent portraits with the calotype created, almost by accident, some impressionistic images. Working in low light and thus having to stretch the process to the

34   The Reverend James Fairbairn and Newhaven fishwives; D. O. Hill and Robert Adamson

35   Highlanders at Edinburgh Castle, D. O. Hill and Robert Adamson

limits of its capabilities, he often produced masterpieces. The low light produced long exposures, too long for his subjects to remain still, and their blurred figures tend to accentuate the grain of the image. Viewing these accidents, he wrote that the soft grainy effect he obtained appealed to him greatly and thereafter he exploited the technique by design. His photographs of the troops at Edinburgh Castle, together with a number of the Newhaven fishermen portraits, are perhaps the first instances of photography being exploited to produce a desired 'impression', rather than tolerated to produce a 'likeness'.

Later, when he returned to photography after Adamson's death, he wrote of his dislike for the collodion process he was then using, preferring the softness and the coarseness of the paper negative, to the clear high-contrast image from the glass plate.

There is little doubt that the genius of Hill and Adamson was not understood, or appreciated, in the 1840s. They enjoyed great success during their short period of collaboration, but that was based primarily on the novelty value of the medium and the relative immediacy of the pictures they produced from their studio on Edinburgh's Calton Hill.

Contemporary artists and critics dismissed the medium as quite unworthy of classification amongst the arts, saying that it was entirely dependent on the sun and an array of boxes and chemicals. The obvious response that the painter was just as dependent on brushes and pigments was not overlooked by the champions of photography.

That the work of photographers such as Hill and Adamson could be dismissed as nothing more than mechanical likenesses is hard to believe, but such is the case. Within a very short time we even find their work being exhibited purely as curios from the early days of photography, and good technical examples of the use of the calotype. That the granularity of the process which appealed to Hill was not appreciated by others is evident in the speed with which the calotype, then free from patent restrictions, was abandoned by photographers throughout the country. Waxed paper too — which had been eagerly taken up by Fenton and many others, was soon out of fashion — by 1857/8 its use was almost unknown.

However, had the history of photography been wholly in the hands of those whose only aim was technical perfection, the subject's heritage would hardly be worthy of our consideration. Luckily, to one side of the progression towards that goal, was a small band of true artists who appreciated the qualities and the challenge of the cruder image and attempted to exploit its unrealised potential. As has been shown, Hill was in the forefront of that small group, and it was an acquaintance of his, also living in Edinburgh, who kept the young tradition of creative photography alive in Scotland in the 1850s, long after the Hill-Adamson partnership had ended.

Thomas Keith, an Edinburgh surgeon who entered photography in 1854 and worked with the medium for only two years, produced a series of pictures using the already outdated waxed paper process which guaranteed his place in history as its finest exponent. Keith was an amateur and, his life uncluttered by the need to capitalise on his skills, he could devote all his energies to producing pictures.

36 Edinburgh — a multiple exposure by Thomas Keith

The granularity of the process and the softness of the image it yielded were, to Thomas Keith, the appeal of waxed paper. He photographed Edinburgh and its environs, working either very early in the morning or very late in the evening to make use of the soft light, and, for the first time, experimented with photography to produce the effects he desired. His pictures of Edinburgh are a testament to his skill, and the print illustrated here, where Keith has produced a multiple exposure on a single paper negative, is, as far as can be ascertained, the first instance of this technique in the development of the medium. For too long his work has been almost unknown outside Scotland. This is soon to be rectified by the publication of a monograph.

At the beginning of this chapter we discussed the problems of changing taste and the need to investigate and discuss the work of the pioneer photographers in terms of Victorian attitudes towards beauty. In looking at the work of the two great professionals, Francis Bedford and Roger Fenton, the position becomes even more complex with the realisation that accepted good taste, and their good taste, were often two entirely different things. Roger Fenton, perhaps photography's first real professional, was capable of both satisfying and offending the artistic tastes of his public, while presumably always producing material which pleased him. In addition, his commercial work for the British Museum, and even some of his architectural work, could vary between the height of artistic and technical achievement, and the totally mundane. The situation is further confused by the fact that, often, what offended his public in the 1850s, is exactly what pleases us today. A prime example of this is the picture 'Terrace and Park, Harewood House'

which was severely criticised in its day for its geometric pattern. Likewise, the near-symmetrical 'Avenue in the Garden, Stonyhurst' appealed little to the Victorian print buyer, and even less to the judges and critics at the various photographic exhibitions of 1859. Where Fenton did achieve recognition was in the realms of the heavy 'still-life' picture, with an endless series of variations on the theme 'Fruit, flowers and Parian Vase'. Nowadays we marvel at their faultless technique but fail to understand their appeal. In 1862, 'for excellence in fruit and flower pieces' Fenton was awarded a medal at the International Exhibition. These images, hailed by his colleagues as being the height of his art, are today considered very definitely of less importance than some of his architectural and landscape material.

Francis Bedford's work was, in general, well received in its day, with the exception of a few excursions into the banal which he, too, made — no doubt for purely commercial reasons. One view of 'The Baptistry, Canterbury Cathedral' which appeared in a folio entitled *The Sunbeam* was, after a lengthy discussion of its content and merit, summed up by its reviewer with the words: 'Next year, Mr Bedford's photograph will be remembered while its title may be forgotten by many . . .' That was praise indeed from the reviewer who, in the next paragraph, summed up a picture by Philip Delamotte by saying 'Magdelen College by Mr Delamotte . . . we should

38   The Terrace and Park, Harewood House, Roger Fenton

prescribe as a punishment for such pictures as this, a three months' excursion among the Alps or Pyrenees with a bad lens and feeble collodion'. (Punishment indeed — life was difficult enough for the wet-plate photographer with a good lens and good collodion!)

The two great portrait photographers featured in this book, Julia Margaret Cameron and Lewis Carroll, have little in common except that they were working at approximately the same time, and in some cases they both photographed the same people. They were also both amateurs.

Julia Margaret Cameron cared little for technique. Her understanding of the collodion process which she used was limited to the absolute minimum necessary to produce a plate which worked. Although this does mean that the quality of her negatives was often poor, she was able to concentrate her attention on the image itself rather than its manufacture. She often claimed that her pictures were not intended to produce a likeness but rather to capture the 'essence' or soul of her sitters. By a mixture of great artistic ability, and a great deal of good luck — her plates were often so badly coated that they really should not have worked — she produced a marvellous series of pictures of her friends and associates from the world of the arts and sciences. Her portrait of Herschel is perhaps one of her most widely known photographs and it is certainly one of her best. The artist

49

39   Coventry, view from the Green, Francis Bedford

40   Suspension bridge, Anglesey, Francis Bedford

George Frederick Watts, the explorer Richard Burton, Tennyson, Browning, Carlyle and Darwin, as well as Alice Liddell — Lewis Carroll's 'Alice in Wonderland — all posed for her camera. That her plates were often covered with dust marks was a sign of her dislike for anything technical, but the soft focus and the blurred effects were created by her own design. She wrote that her intention was 'to overcome realism by diminishing just in the least degree, the precision of the focus'. Mrs Cameron's famous friends did not merely pose for her out of friendship, but also out of a real respect and admiration for her work. 'I wish I could paint such a picture as this' wrote George Frederick Watts of one of her photographs.

Lewis Carroll (Charles Lutwidge Dodgson) had Mrs Cameron's love of the artistic. His appreciation of fine art and nature were not matched by a skill to sketch or paint, so photography was the natural outlet for his skills. He was, however, a perfectionist and, unlike Mrs Cameron, tried to become as technically proficient as possible. His pictures are in a totally different vein to those produced by his more famous contemporary, although this should not be taken as a guide to their relative positions in the lists of the best Victorian portrait photographers. While becoming famous as a writer, and especially as the creator of Alice, Lewis Carroll quietly progressed to a position in the ranks of the top six portrait photographers of his time. His

41   Betws y Coed, Francis Bedford

42   Sir John Herschell, Julia Margaret Cameron

43   'La Contadina', Julia Margaret Cameron

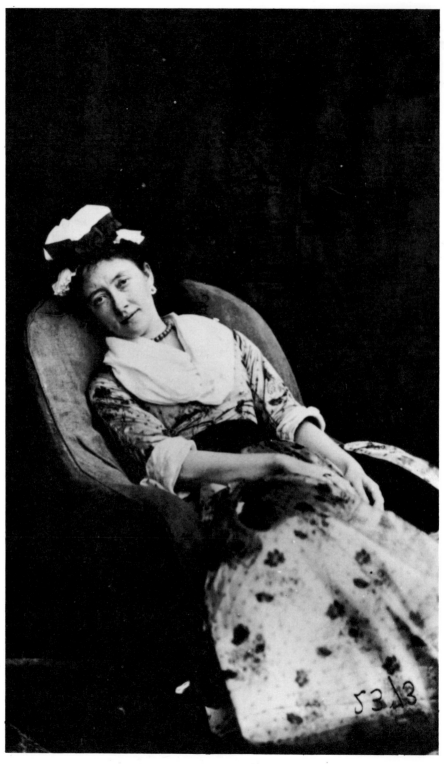

44   Marion Terry, Lewis Carroll

45   Alice and her sister in Chinese costume, Lewis Carroll

patience in first learning the techniques of collodion, and then working towards the perfection he desired, has resulted in a superb set of intimate and totally sympathetic portraits of his colleagues. Their quality speaks for itself.

Lake Price in his *Manual of Photographic Manipulation* in 1868 spent a great deal of time on the aesthetics of portrait photography — one area at least where the same criteria were used to judge the painting and the photograph. He wrote:

> In portraiture, the student should refer to prints from the works of Velazquez, Titian, Vandyke, Rembrandt, Rubens, our own Gainsborough and Sir Joshua Reynolds, eschewing the affections of the periwig school of Mignard and Lely. If he really can do anything, this study will surely bear fruit and make itself felt in his works. It has lately been a matter of observation how much the study of art principles has enabled Mr Adam Salomon to prove the fallacy of the idea that the photographic representation is a mere mechanism, dependent upon the lens and the box it is mounted in, whereas in this department of it, and in all that is arranged and composed from the human figure, the will, the intention, and the idiosyncracy of the producer makes itself felt as completely as though he were at work with palette and brushes.

55

46   Pike fishing, Loch of Park, George Washington Wilson

Even Lake Price did not concede at that point that the 'will, the intention, and the idiosyncracy of the producer' made itself felt in other branches of photography!

In the first edition of his book, published ten years earlier, he had looked forward to the production of landscapes 'of greater artistic excellence and interest', but had felt that this would be only possible when the process was more refined and the facility for 'instantaneous' pictures had been realised. It seems to have been a logical assumption in his mind that 'artistic excellence' could not be acheived with the process in its rather cruder state in 1858. There does appear to have been this belief that 'artistic excellence' and completely faithful reproduction were one and the same thing.

It is true to say, however, that the simpler the process became, the easier it was for the non-technically minded photographer to operate in the medium and, therefore, concentrate entirely on the composition of the image rather than its manufacture. As photography progressed away from its earliest and crudest form, the mere production of a picture ceased to be worthy of note. The photographers were expected to contribute a little more to their work than the mere physical fact of completing a journey through a sequence of mechanical events.

The growth in the number of photographers on the scene also had its effect. With the advent of the small cheap photograph, those who remained working in the large format had to be good to justify their continued existence. George Washington Wilson, who was already established in the field of stereoscopic photography, extended the range of photography by producing the first photographs in which the sun itself, rather than just its reflected

56

47 'Gathering Waterlilies', P. H. Emerson

sparkle, actually appeared. His 'Loch of Park' and 'Oban, Sunset' were milestones of landscape photography, beautifully composed, perfectly executed and, quite justifiably, were classed even by his contemporaries as equalling the finest achievements of the artists.

The problems encountered by those photographers who did attempt to approach photography as they might have approached painting, were not merely those directly involved with the process with which they were working. Their colleagues placed such restrictions upon what was or was not permitted in the name of art that the cause of 'picture making' within photography was severely hampered. The leading pictorialist H. P. Robinson was frowned upon for his pioneering work in photomontage — the art of piecing together several photographs to produce one large complete picture. His 'Gathering in the May' was produced from seven or eight negatives and his 'A Cottage Home', too, was a montage. Oscar Rejlander pioneered the production of combination prints and his best known work, 'Two ways of Life', was the result of literally dozens of individual negatives and hours of careful matching and printing. So severe were the restrictions that the purists in photography attempted to impress upon their contemporaries that Robinson was even criticised (by Thomas Sutton, Editor of *Photographic Notes*) for adding a heavy thunderous sky to a coastal scene. Reports of exhibitions were full of pompous complaining prose on the sins of producing the unreal. One print, also by Robinson, which had received a favourable report in one edition of *Photographic Notes* and was subsequently found to be a montage, was condemned a few weeks later. Although any method of obtaining the desired effect in painting was permissible, in photography

57

tolerance of experimentation was noticeable only by its absence. The pictorialists and romanticists were not only condemned by the technicians in photography — they also had to contend with fierce criticisms from another group — the naturalistic photographers.

By the 1870s and 1880s, when Frank Meadow Sutcliffe was working in Whitby, and Peter Henry Emerson was working in Norfolk, an appreciation of creative photography was in a much more advanced state of development. These men and their contemporaries had much more freedom to exploit whatever means was at their disposal in order to achieve their aims. Emerson's magnificent 'Gathering Waterlilies' is a good example of just how well he succeeded. Here, at last, is the true artist at work with a camera.

Emerson's work was a reaction against the heavy Victorian 'tableau' — the penchant for dressing up in photographs and assuming that the contrived is artistic. In his book *Naturalistic Photography* he called for the same return to nature in photography which painting had made in the late eighteenth century. As there were no pictures in his book he compiled *Pictures of East Anglian Life*, a series of photographs produced within the limitations of the text of *Naturalistic Photography*. He set out to prove to photographers that if they looked to nature for their subjects, they would find a simple beauty which lent itself perfectly to the medium in which they were working. Using the platinotype process, and working only when the light was absolutely right for his purpose, Emerson produced seven of the finest collections of photographs ever taken. *Life and Landscape of the Norfolk Broads*, perhaps the

48 'The Basket Maker', P. H. Emerson

finest of the seven, is the book from which the pictures illustrated here are drawn.

The platinotype process mentioned above may need a little explanation. It was invented by William Willis in 1873, and was an attempt at producing a permanent print. Silver prints are not completely stable when produced under normal conditions and can fade. Platinum, being a more stable metal, seemed a more suitable basis for a permanent printing paper. Willis's Platinotype Company first manufactured pre-sensitised platinum paper in 1880 and it achieved almost overnight success. Emerson used the paper more for the subtlety of tones it produced than for the archival permanence that it offered. The image was capable of very delicate mid-tones, offering Emerson a more natural softness for his naturalistic pictures.

Sutcliffe, in Whitby, was turning his eye and camera on the people and the sights of his native town. His skill for composition and his simplicity of style produced a unique record of a small fishing town. His pictures, thanks to his totally sympathetic treatment of the town, and the elements which played upon it, give the viewer an almost intimate knowledge of the place.

Ten years later, in the 1890s, the whole scene changed. With the advent of a number of photographers who saw the medium as another tool in the hands of the artist, rather than as a glorified recording instrument, an appreciation of the work of many of the pioneers began to emerge. No longer were the best of Fenton's pictures, Hill's pictures and the work of others

49 'Snipe Shooting', P. H. Emerson

50 'A Bit of News', Frank Meadow Sutcliffe

51 'Sunshine and Shadow', Frank Meadow Sutcliffe

52 'An Unwilling Pupil', Frank Meadow Sutcliffe

merely regarded as good photographs, they were appreciated as *pictures*. Photo-impressionism, which attracted the attention of Glasgow photographer Thomas Annan, also drew attention to the hitherto almost ignored qualities of Hill's pictures.

In praising the delightful harmony and balance in Sutcliffe's 'An Unwilling Pupil', they looked again at Fenton's equally appealing 'Cookhouse of the 8th Hussars', a masterpiece of group portraiture produced nearly forty years before.

Photography towards the end of the century reached the level of high art, mainly due, perhaps, to the fact that the mundane side of the business was, more and more, falling into the hands of the Kodak-equipped amateur. The establishment of photography as a fine art, developing alongside a more commercial approach to the subject, but quite independent of it, set a pattern which has survived to this day.

Part Two: The Photographers

David Octavius Hill (1802-70) and Robert Adamson (1821-48)

D. O. Hill was nineteen years old when, in 1821, his future collaborator, Robert Adamson was born. Hill was the son of a Perth bookseller, and with the family's background in the world of printing and publishing it was not surprising that his artistic talents were channelled into sketching and lithography.

From his early teens Hill published collections of lithographs. *Sketches of Scenery in Perthshire* was the first of a series of publications and professional assignments he completed, which included lithographic engravings to illustrate the works of Scott, Burns and others, and also a series of sketches to adorn the pages of the Glasgow and Garnkirk Railway Company's timetable. A founder member of the Royal Scottish Academy, and in the 1830s its secretary, Hill was a frequent exhibitor at galleries in central Scotland and especially in Edinburgh where he lived. His reputation as a painter spread rapidly, bringing him substantial sales and a seemingly endless stream of lithographic work.

In 1843, a memorable year for him, Hill witnessed the disruption of the Church of Scotland and the setting up of the Free Church. Either by commission or personal choice he embarked on the long task of producing a huge painting to commemorate the occasion. The work involved was enormous, and at the suggestion of Sir David Brewster, one of Scotland's photographic pioneers, Hill decided to learn the calotype process of photography. By photographing all the dissenting ministers, and working from the paper prints, he could greatly reduce the work involved in the production of the 'Disruption Picture'. Brewster taught him the basics of the process and also introduced him to a young engineer, Robert Adamson who could help him in the work. That introduction marked the beginning of what is perhaps the most successful partnership in the history of photography.

For almost a year Hill and Adamson turned their camera towards the production of the hundreds of portraits needed for the painting. With the ministers appearing before the lens either singly or in groups, a series of over sixty calotypes was produced, recording for posterity the 450 founders of the Free Church.

The two men's interest in photograph grew rapidly and even overtook Hill's ambition to produce the painting. Travelling to Durham, St Andrews and further afield, they photographed the traditional and the unique, the places and the people of Scotland in the 1840s. The fishermen and women of Newhaven, the troops at Edinburgh Castle, the artists and the writers, were all subjected to a minute of immobility in front of the camera. The

63

53   St Sálvator's Church, St Andrews

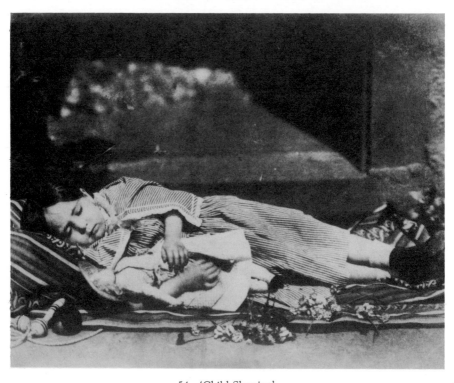

54   'Child Sleeping'

55   Greyfriar's Churchyard

results were a series of photographs of unequalled brilliance and a unique record of their era. In their photographs Edinburgh's now blackened Scott Monument was a strange, partially built structure of pale stone. Greyfriar's churchyard was a hive of activity, and the now quiet quays of Newhaven and St Andrews were bustling with activity.

Tragically, Adamson died in 1848 at the age of only twenty-seven, after less than five years in photography. Without his partner, and a little disillusioned at the speed with which calotypes faded, Hill abandoned photography and resumed his career as an artist. He later made a return to the art with a Glasgow photographer by the name of McGlashan, but found little satisfaction in the wet-plate process.

His return to painting, an art form at which he excelled, marked the end of photography's first great partnership, and Hill's failure to reach the artistic heights, either on his own or with others, which he had achieved with Adamson, is a testament to the latter's genius.

Roger Fenton (1819-69)

Roger Fenton's father, a successful Lancashire mill-owner, sat for a short time in the house of Commons as MP for Rochdale. Across the floor of the house from him sat Fox Talbot as MP for Chippenham. Before the emergence of Roger as a photographer, that was the nearest the family had ever been to photography!

Fenton's early years were set against a background of immense wealth — the family fortunes were on the ascent all through the first half of the nineteenth century — and it was therefore far from necessary that Roger should seek a profitable career. He trained first as an artist under Paul 'from today painting is dead' Delaroche and then as a solicitor.

Once established in his legal career Roger Fenton turned to photography

56　Balaclava, the cattle pier

as a hobby, using the waxed paper process, and became a founder member of the Calotype Club. In 1852, with his friend the engineer Charles Vignoles, Fenton went to Russia, returning with a fine series of pictures including the now-famous 'Domes of the Cathedral of the Resurrection' taken in the Kremlin. In 1853 he became deeply involved in the formation of the Photographic Society — now the Royal Photographic Society — and was subsequently elected as its secretary. In later years he served as vice-president and was instrumental in the development of what has become the premier photographic society in the world.

In 1854 Fenton started a long association with the British Museum. His high quality work earned him high fees as the museum's official photographer, a post he retained for many years. In that same year he produced the first photographs of the Royal Family, and taught the Prince Consort the basic elements of photography. 1854 also saw the beginning of the Crimean war and, with Fenton's sponsored expedition to the Crimea in the following year, the start of the modern photographic coverage of wars. His pictures were the result of financial backing by Thomas Agnew, the Manchester print publishers, and the expedition had the unofficial blessing of the War Department and Lord Newcastle.

The Photo-Galvanographic Company gave Fenton another outlet for his talent. He was appointed their chief photographer in 1856, and, although that association was rather short-lived, it has left us with yet further proof of the all-round professionalism of this great photographer.

With the advent of the stereo-boom in the late 1850s, Fenton was, once again, at the centre of things; the *Stereoscopic Magazine* and the *Stereoscopic*

57 'Valley of the Shadow of Death'

67

58 Cathedral of the Resurrection, Kremlin

Cabinet frequently became the shopwindows for his latest productions.

Fenton is remembered today primarily for the Crimean pictures and his superb architectural and landscape work, but he would perhaps be better remembered simply as a *professional* who, for only a little more than a decade, was one of the driving forces of British photography.

With his great involvement in the medium it was all the more surprising that he decided in 1862 to retire completely from photography. His decision was made quickly and, as if to remove temptation completely, he sold all his equipment, together with thousands of glass negatives and albumen prints. He had been using the collodion process since the Crimean expedition and it was his very knowledge of that process which had prompted Agnew to choose him for the task.

Fenton died in 1869. Many of his photographs were bought by Francis Frith's publishing company in Reigate. They brought out a series of folio volumes entitled *The Works of Roger Fenton* which were bought by an eager public. Other pictures appeared, overprinted with the legend *F. F. & Co* in a series of tourist booklets and, even more surprisingly, one of his pictures 'A View on the Hodder' was still in current production as a postcard in 1970!

Julia Margaret Cameron (1815-79)

'When I have had such men before my camera, my whole soul has endeavoured to do its duty towards them in recording faithfully the greatness of

59 'The Day Dream'

the inner as well as the features of the outer man. The photograph thus taken has been almost the embodiment of a prayer'.

In those few words Mrs Cameron, who became involved with photography for the first time at the age of forty-eight, summed up her approach to the subject in her book *Annals of My Glasshouse*. The glasshouse was a common sight in the garden of the Victorian photographer. Such was the need for good clear light that most photographers had large glass structures specially constructed. Mrs Cameron, true to her ideal of total involvement, was no exception, and the glasshouse was duly constructed in the garden of her home at Freshwater in the Isle of Wight.

Photography and Mrs Cameron had come together to alleviate the latter's boredom during the frequent and extended absences of her husband overseas. Her friend Sir John Herschel taught her the collodion process — or at least the absolute basics of the process — and she talked her eminent friends into doing duty as models. Her favourite photographer, Oscar Rejlander, was summoned to Freshwater to help her and to discuss the 'black art' with her, or, as she herself expressed it, 'to help with his great experience'.

Her penchant for producing the 'tableau vivant' type of picture meant that many of her literary and artistic friends were almost unrecognisable in her photographs, so heavy and elaborate were the disguises. Her servant, Mary Hilliers, appeared in so many photographs in the guise of the Virgin Mary, that her more familiar name around the house became 'Mary Madonna'. Tennyson spent many hours in the glasshouse before Mrs Cameron produced the desired picture of 'The Dirty Monk'. Even her own children answered the call of duty and, in 'Venus Chiding Cupid', produced one of Mrs Cameron's most successful and certainly most sentimental pictures.

Her friendship with Tennyson blossomed into a strange sort of association, and one outcome was her series of illustrations of his works. 'Idylls of the King', her first series of images from poetry, echoes the experiments carried out by Hill and Adamson years before. Hill's portrayal of the sculptor John Henning as 'Edie Ochiltree' from Scott's *The Antiquary* cannot escape comparison with Mrs Cameron's 'The Passing of Arthur'. The repeated attempts by photography to be accepted as art by imitation, rather than originality, is the one facet of Victorian photography which is hard to understand. Mrs Cameron's love of the tableau produced such heavily sentimental pictures as 'Pray God, bring father safely home' which, although very well received in its day, is as alien to us today as Roger Fenton's 'Hush lightly tread. Still tranquility she sleeps' produced a few years earlier.

Mrs Cameron and Lewis Carroll shared a number of subjects in their photography; Mrs Cameron photographed Alice Liddell as 'Alathea', a few years after Carroll. Her photographs of Ellen Terry — who later married Julia Margaret's close friend George Frederick Watts — were also taken several years after Lewis Carroll's portraits of the entire Terry family.

The surviving portraits by Julia Margaret Cameron make it quite obvious that her technical knowledge was minimal — cracked varnish on her negatives and dust on the collodion (itself unevenly coated) prove that her enthusiasm was directed entirely towards the actual image. Luckily — for

60   Alice Liddell

61   Mrs Herbert Duckworth

many of her original prints faded and stained quickly — much of her work was reprinted later by others. Her lighting techniques were years ahead of their time. Not for her the omnidirectional light found in most glasshouses — Mrs Cameron controlled the light carefully, caring little for the comfort of her sitters in holding these long poses. Somehow, as if appreciating the genius of the woman, all her subjects tolerated her impositions. The result was a series of brilliant portraits which brought Victorian portraiture out of oblivion and into the ranks of high art.

Francis Bedford (1816-94)

In turning to the work of Francis Bedford we turn towards one of the most respected figures of mid-nineteenth century photography. Bedford, a perfectionist as well as a fine artist, was responsible for a large number of photographic masterpieces. He is an enigmatic figure; very little is known of his life and work and, sadly, his photographs do not receive the wide appreciation today which they merit.

A lithographer by training, Bedford was well established in the art world long before he ever contemplated taking up photography. From the early 1840s he had been publishing books and wallcharts on the general theme of ornament, which took in everything from the simple embellishment of a page of a book, to the decorated styles of church architecture. His first full-length book, and the publication which established him in the front lines of lithography, was *The Industrial Arts of the 19th Century*, written by M. D. Wyatt, but illustrated with 160 of Bedford's finest lithographs. These ornate coloured lithographic prints made the book a treasured possession.

The Treasure of Ornament and *The Treasury of Ornamental Art* led Bedford to a commission to illustrate the catalogue for the 1857 Manchester Art Treasures Exhibition, one of the major art exhibitions of the nineteenth century. With that catalogue providing more than adequate proof of his immense skills, Bedford's work was in great demand.

However well his lithographic reputation may have been established, it was about that time that he began to work with the wet collodion process and, from 1857 onwards, mentions in the photographic press assure us that he was as successful in his new interest as he had been in his first. If we are to believe the reports of the time, technical and artistic excellence in his work was the rule rather than the exception.

His skills with photographic equipment led him to be asked to test new lenses, and often pieces of equipment which had been written off as useless by others, were used to produce masterpieces in the hands of Francis Bedford. In short, he was quickly recognised as one of the masters of his craft, and that recognition led, in 1862, to a Royal Command to accompany the Prince of Wales on his tour of the Near East. This was not the first time he had responded to the royal command, for in 1854 he had worked for Dr Becker,

62   View from the Ketschenbrucke, Coburg, 1857

63   A group taken during the Middle East tour of the Prince of Wales, 1862

64 On the suspension bridge, Anglesey

the Prince's secretary and tutor, producing a number of photographs of royal treasures. Many of those, it must be said, are not of the quality of his later photographs. At the same time Roger Fenton was working for the Queen and Prince, turning out work of a much higher quality. Ten years later, however, Fenton, reading reviews of exhibitions, would find several suggestions from critics that he might learn a little from Mr Bedford on technique and composition!

On his return from the Near East — and from what the Prince had mentioned in his diary as a very fruitful photographic expedition — Francis Bedford's photographs were published in a series of volumes by the London publishers Day & Son of Lincoln's Inn Fields. Surprisingly, as far as we have been able to ascertain — and in direct contrast to Roger Fenton's published series of prints — no volumes of the Bedford pictures survive. At 43 guineas for the 21 volumes containing a total of 175 pictures, they were less expensive than Fenton's Crimean pictures but, perhaps, the subjects were less attractive to the print-buying public, and were not looked after as carefully as they might have been. The series of pictures gave Bedford the basis of a collection of archaeological and historical subjects, which he subsequently expanded to form the illustrations for a number of books in the years which followed his return from the Holy Land. After 1870 no more books appeared, although much of his photographic material, like Fenton's, appears to have finished up with Francis Frith, who continued to publish it for decades.

George Washington Wilson (1823-93)

In his book *A Manual of Photographic Manipulation* Lake Price wrote of the photographer's dream of instant pictures. His comment was timely, for, in that same year, 1858, George Washington Wilson achieved that ambition. He worked from a studio in Aberdeen and for decades was one of Britain's most important photographers yet, surprisingly, very few people have ever come across his name. He, more than any other pioneer, has a just claim to be in the forefront of Victorian photography.

With a single exposure in the bustle of Princes Street in Edinburgh in 1858, George Washington Wilson gave photography its first 'snapshot', although that term meant more in his day than it does now. His was the first exposure to be made 'instantly', as opposed to the many seconds used by his contemporaries. Fenton's exposures were in the order of one to five seconds, others took even longer — (Francis Frith liked at least forty-five seconds' exposure so he could stop his lens well down) — but Wilson, with a great deal of ingenuity, produced fine pictures with an exposure of one sixth of a second.

His technique made ingenious use of his glengarry bonnet. With one hand he removed the lens cap and with the other he covered the lens with his bonnet, taking one sixth of a second for the entire operation. These were the

65   Regent Street, London

66 Queen Victoria

days before shutters were invented and the normal exposure technique was to remove the lens cap, count the required number of seconds for the exposure and then replace the cap.

George Washington Wilson was born in Banffshire and in his early twenties began to establish a reputation as a miniature painter of some note. He had turned to photography by the early 1850s and by 1856 had been appointed Photographer Royal to Queen Victoria while she was in Scotland. This obviously enhanced his reputation but, even without that honour, his pictures would have earned him a fine enough reputation on their own. His skill with the small format stereo camera produced some of the finest landscape pictures of his era. Thomas Sutton, the often-critical editor of *Photographic Notes*, could rarely find a harsh word to say about Wilson's photography. Almost every issue of the magazine seems to contain a glowing report on 'Mr Wilson's new pictures'. The surprise with which many of his photographs were received, reflects the fact that the public was just not used to seeing the bustle of life in photographs. The long exposures always made streets look empty — people moving quickly across the frame were not recorded on the plate. When the Princes Street series was first shown, the comment was 'how infinitely superior to those "cities of the dead" with which we have hitherto had to content ourselves'. The small stereo plate required a shorter exposure than the larger landscape plates, but it would still not have been short enough to give instant pictures had not Wilson also experimented with the use of iron protosulphate as a developer for his collodion plates, instead of the usual pyrogallic acid. The 'iron development' process had been known since 1851, but it was not until Wilson arrived on the scene that its full potential was realised.

As well as being a fine artist, Wilson was also a technical perfectionist. Although he bought his equipment 'off the shelf', he spent hours modifying his cameras and lenses in order to cut down flare, improve the handling characteristics and thus improve the quality of the pictures he would be able to take. He was also disturbed by the 'frilling' which was a feature of collodion plates — the collodion would fray around the edges thus spoiling the overall appearance of the picture. He therefore worked with larger plates — 9 in × $4\frac{1}{2}$ in (for two stereo pictures) — and printed only the central areas. He contrived, therefore, to remove the areas of frilling and blemishes.

Had George Washington Wilson contributed only his skills as a photographer, we would still hold him in high regard. But, he was just as efficient as a salesman and, over the years, built up a publishing concern which, with two huge factories in Aberdeen, soon rivalled, and perhaps even overtook, the mammoth Francis Frith enterprise in Reigate. Wilson was a progressive. His ideas were well ahead of his contemporaries and perhaps decades ahead of the technical capabilities of photography. He pioneered many ideas in photography and certainly considered one more, which would not be realised in his lifetime. He wrote, in *Photographic Notes* in 1861: 'I have never given up the idea that we shall be able to photograph in colours some day by following out the right path . . . and if you think me crack-brained I shall arrange them [his ideas] someday and submit them to your criticism'.

67 Shipwreck by George Washington Wilson

Lewis Carroll (1832-98)

Through the Looking-glass is an apt title both for the second *Alice* book by Lewis Carroll, and for the photographic activities of Charles Lutwidge Dodgson. His whole story is fascinating. Had his dual-character been the creation of a fiction writer, then we, the readers, would have found it hard to believe. He was an eminent mathematician and a keen amateur photographer, but he would never admit to being Lewis Carroll. He even went as far as issuing a statement which said: 'Mr Dodgson neither claims nor acknowledges any connection with the books not published under his name', and he claimed only to have written works of mathematics such as *Euclid and His Modern Rivals* published in 1879, thirteen years after *Alice's Adventures in Wonderland* and seven years after *Through the Looking-glass*.

He may have disliked any association between his 'Lewis Carroll' works and his mathematical writings, but there is very little doubt that it was his Carroll personality which became really involved in photography. His photographs of Alice are the obvious link. Perhaps it was Dodgson the mathematician who tackled the technicalities of the process, and Carroll the artist who composed the pictures.

68　Portrait of Lewis Carroll

69 Alice Liddell and her sisters

He delighted in photographing children, especially little girls under the age of sixteen, in whose faces he captured a rare timeless moment which was at once both delicate and feminine, mischievous and alluring. In Alice and her sisters, Ellen Terry and her sisters, and a number of other girls, Carroll found faces which, through his looking-glass, could be interpreted and recorded for ever. The portraits he produced were true masterpieces and, like Alice herself, have become eternal. Alice, photographed by Carroll when she was a little girl, was photographed again later by Mrs Cameron. That picture, of a beautiful elegant young lady, was a far cry from the child in Chinese costume of a decade earlier.

70   Ellen Terry

71   The Reverend Richard Meux Benson

Lewis Carroll has been portrayed in photographic histories as a true amateur who never sold any of his photographs. The truth, however, is quite the opposite. On several occasions he wrote of selling twenty prints and more of a single picture in one day. Perhaps he never took photographs for purely commercial reasons, but he certainly does appear to have earned money as a result of his endeavours.

When he first became involved in photography, Dodgson was a Fellow of Christ Church, Oxford. His first camera, bought in 1856 from Ottewill, the London manufacturer who equipped most of the leading photographers of the day, cost £15 — an enormous sum for a complete novice in the art. With his friend, the poet Robert Southey, to explain to him the intricacies of the wet-plate process, Dodgson set about the task of mastering the equipment. For a quarter of a century photography was his major hobby. Without the aid of 'photographic vans' or carriages, he trundled his huge camera and its processing equipment around the country wherever he went. While his architectural and landscape photographs were as good as any being produced by his contemporaries, it was his portraits which formed the basis of his great reputation as a photographer. His work in photography must rank equal in importance to his writing. It is a nice thought that Lewis Carroll's photography is directly responsible for *Alice in Wonderland*, for it was while looking for models for his photography that he first met Dean Liddell's little daughter, then just four years old.

Frank Meadow Sutcliffe (1853-1941)

Robert Adamson had been dead for five years and Roger Fenton had, along with others, formed the Photographic Society before Frank Sutcliffe was even born. Many advances had been made in photography before Sutcliffe became involved in professional portraiture around 1875. The speed of the wet collodion plates (which he used for his first five years as a photographer) had been greatly increased and, as a result, the relatively informal portrait or group photograph was becoming commonplace.

What Sutcliffe did for photography was, quite simply, to use the medium to better effect than ever before. In his native town of Whitby, he produced a unique and impressive documentation of the life and times of one small town, which was already being left behind by the rest of the world.

Whitby, a small fishing and one-time whaling port on the east coast, was, by virtue of its remote position, an unhurried town — its people still living life in a way which the more industrialised centres had completely abandoned by the 1880s. Frank Sutcliffe painstakingly recorded that way of life with a simple approach to photography which, at the same time, was being preached by Emerson in Norfolk. Naturalistic photography, as Emerson called the approach of both men, was a complete rejection of the contrivance of earlier photographers and proved that man and nature were the ideal subjects.

72 'Weekly News'

Frank Sutcliffe's pictures — which span half a century — capture the essence of life in Whitby and are of immense value as historical documents. Many of them, especially those produced while the photographer was in his twenties, are also magnificent works of art. His skill in capturing the casual, the touching, the endearing and the sad, provided history with perhaps the first series of completely natural portraits. His landscapes, particularly scenes at farms near Whitby, have a living quality which make them seem almost ready to jump out of the frame — and the technical quality seems to deny the fact that these pictures were taken nearly a century ago.

Sutcliffe would go to great lengths to capture the exact moment he was looking for. Waiting for up to a quarter of an hour for the pose, the expression he needed, he would moisten his darkslides to keep the wet collodion plate damp — had the plate dried, of course, its sensitivity would have been greatly reduced. His approach was akin to that of the modern photographer — in that he waited for the precise moment when the subject's expression pleased him — rather than the traditional Victorian practice of posing the picture long before the plate was even coated. Sutcliffe's approach could be likened to a 'snapshot' photographer, and he himself wrote in 1875 'quietly watch your subjects as they are working or playing . . . and whenever you see a nice arrangement . . . say "Keep still just as you are a quarter of a minute", and expose, instead of placing an arm here a foot there . . .'

His ideal was to record the natural, never to attempt to imitate the natural in forced poses. In images such as 'Water Rats', 'A Bit of News' and the

73 'Water Rats'

superb study 'An Unwilling Pupil', the degree to which his approach paid off is undeniable. These pictures are by no means exceptional in comparison with his other work. They are merely representative of the great skill of Frank Sutcliffe. In his work we see, perhaps for the first time, a photographer who is an artist, not merely in background, but in his approach to the subject. The early masters of Victorian photography were bound to be influenced to

74   Henry Freeman

some degree by the novelty of the process. By Sutcliffe's day the novelty value was minimal and the technical capabilities of the process much greater. Frank Sutcliffe used the process as a painter might use paints and canvas, and his work exhibits both technical and artistic skills of the highest order. The artistic skill is apparent in the images, and the technical can be appreciated when the reader learns that the examples of his work in this book have all been printed from the original 8½ in × 6½ in negatives, taken nearly a century ago.

Peter Henry Emerson (1856-1936)

There is no doubt that if the title of 'Father of Naturalistic Photography' was to be applied to any of the photographic artists who sprang to prominence in the 1880s, then that honour would go to Emerson — for he coined the phrase.

'From today, painting is dead' had been the exclamation of Paul Delaroche when he saw his first photograph, but perhaps 'from today taste is dead' might have been a more apt comment. Rather than the expected prominence of fine art photography, the first half-century had been marked by a combination of 'photography for photography's sake' and sheer over-emotional bad taste. Almost every photographer had been guilty of the sin at some time in his career.

We have already commented in earlier chapters on the restrictions placed on those who saw photography as another medium in which the artist might express himself. For decades the restrictions remained, until the emergence of Cuban-born Peter Emerson finally drove them into oblivion.

Emerson began to seriously involve himself in photography in his mid-thirties. His approach was that of a student — he examined all that had been produced and all that was being produced at that time — and, convinced that photography was indeed an art form, set about defining his approach to it.

Emerson, however, not only revolted against the technicians in photography, but also against the pictorialists who, in his view, were as guilty in their contrivance as the sentimentalists were in theirs. Robinson received only disapproval for his approach, while the work of Oscar Rejlander (who was already dead by the time of Emerson's entry into photography) hardly warranted a comment. Photography's repeated attempts to copy painting in order to be classed as a fine art particularly disgusted Emerson. The pictorialists were perfectionists as far as photographic technique was concerned — their lenses stopped down completely for maximum sharpness. Their poses were solid and steady and fitted neatly into pre-conceived painterly compositions. Emerson rejected all that, setting out to record nature and life in as natural a manner as possible. He photographed often slightly out of focus to achieve softness, and his pictures were always truth-

75 'A Winter's Morning'

76 'In the Barley Harvest'

ful — he never adapted what he saw to suit his own requirements. If the scene was not as he wished it, he waited, often for long periods of time, until, like Sutcliffe, he recorded on his plate exactly the image which nature had presented.

His approach to photography, and the doctrines he preached, caused a great split in photographic thinking, but he backed up his beliefs with a series of folios of his work, starting with *Life and Landscape on the Norfolk Broads* in 1886 and culminating with *Marsh Leaves* in 1895.

In 1889 he published a book entitled *Naturalistic Photography* in which he expressed all his conclusions and beliefs about photography as an art form, using his folios as the illustrations. His writings, although rejected by many, must have seemed like a breath of fresh air to others, and many photographers throughout the country applauded them. However, claiming to have been convinced that he was wrong by an unnamed painter, he produced a brochure the following year in which he withdrew all his statements of 1889. *The Death of Naturalistic Photography*, as the leaflet was entitled, did not noticeably affect his own photography and certainly did little to convince those moved by the first book.

The pamphlet, edged in black, and containing an epitaph which is quite

77 'A Stiff Pull'

clear in its aims — 'Naturalistic photography . . . brought out the low morality of certain persons in the photographic world . . .' — was perhaps Emerson's personal epitaph. In it he was really lamenting his own withdrawal from a position of prominence in photography. In the year which followed his publication, Emerson watched from the wings as his disciples, including George Davidson, sat down and discussed photography with the pictorialists. They eventually emerged in 1892 as the 'Linked Ring', a brotherhood embracing the opposites of photographic art and artists — including pictorialism and naturalistic photography, Robinson and Davidson.

Perhaps he foresaw this dramatic link being forged and, knowing full well that he could never bring himself to accept anything outside the narrow confines of his own rules, he gave up. His naturalistic movement had, in a way, failed in its aim of destroying pictorialism. He had hoped that he could establish photography as an art without embracing the many facets of the subject which he despised. As might have been expected, photography's claim to be classed as an art was all-embracing. What he had achieved, however, was two-fold. He, personally, had widened the scope of photography by laying down simple rules which are as appropriate today as in 1889. He also produced some of the finest images in the history of photography.

In *Naturalistic Photography*, he underlined the discipline required in photography '. . . I would express upon all beginners, the necessity for beginning work with a clear distinction between the aims and ends of Science and Art. When the art student has acquired enough knowledge — that is *Science* — to express what he wishes, let him, with jealous care, keep the scientific mental attitude, if I may so express it, far away'.

In Emerson's hands photography started to move away from a situation where the photograph needed explanation, where a reviewer at an exhibition would feel obliged to tell his readers of the problems the photographer encountered with his collodion, his lens or his nitrate bath. From now on, the picture could be judged entirely on its visual merits.

Bibliography

Books and Catalogues

Arts Council. *From Today Painting Is Dead* (London, 1971)

Gernsheim, Helmut. *Creative Photography—Aesthetic Trends 1839-1960* (London, 1962)

————. *History of Photography* (London, 1969)

————. *Lewis Carroll, Photographer* (New York, 1969)

————. *Julia Margaret Cameron* (New York, 1974)

Hannavy, John. *Roger Fenton of Crimble Hall* (London, 1974)

Hiley, Michael. *Frank Meadow Sutcliffe* (London, 1974)

Life Library of Photography (Amsterdam, 1971)

Lyons, Nathan. *Photographers on Photography* (New York, 1966)

Newhall, Beaumont. *History of Photography* (New York, 1964)

Ovenden, Graham. *A Victorian Album* (London, 1975)

Science Museum Catalogue (London, 1969)

Scottish Arts Council Catalogue. Hannavy, John. 'A Camera Goes to War' (Edinburgh, 1974)

————. Michaelson, Katherine. 'David Octavius Hill and Robert Adamson' (Edinburgh, 1970)

Shaw, Bill Eglon. *Frank Meadow Sutcliffe: Photographs* (Whitby, 1974)

Thomas, D. B. *The First Negatives* (London, 1964)

Turner, Peter and Wood, Richard. *P. H. Emerson, Photographer of Norfolk* (London, 1974)

Journals and Books

The Photographic Journal, 1853-80

Photographic News

Photographic News Almanac

Photographic Notes, 1856-62

Acknowledgements

The publishers are indebted to the following for permission to reproduce photographs:
Aberdeen City Libraries for nos 18, 46, 65, 66, 67; The British Theatre Museum for nos 44,
70; Colman and Rye Libraries of Local History, Norwich County Libraries for nos 47, 48, 49,
75, 76, 77; The Earl of Harewood for no 38; Edinburgh City Libraries for no 36; Kodak
Museum for no 21; Manchester City Libraries for no 32; The Mansell Collection for nos 45,
60, 69; National Galleries of Scotland for no 35; The National Portrait Gallery for nos 68, 71;
Rochdale Libraries for no 33; The Royal Archives (by gracious permission of HM
The Queen(for nos 62, 63; The Science Museum for nos 1, 2, 3, 5, 6, 8, 9, 10, 13, 14, 15, 16,
17, 34, 39, 40, 41, 42, 43, 53, 54, 55, 56, 57, 59, 61, 64; The Science Museum, Crown
copyright for nos 4, 7; Scottish United Services Museum for nos 19, 58; The Stonyhurst
Collection for nos 20, 37; The Sutcliffe Gallery for nos 50, 51, 52, 72, 73, 74; William Tayler
for nos 11, 12. All photographs not otherwise acknowledged are from the author's collection.

Index

(Titles of books and photographs are printed in italics.)